ALEJANDRO MAYORKAS IN THE HOT SEAT

Charting the Course of American History with the First Cabinet Impeachment in 150 Years

Freeman Trends

Table Of Contents

ALEJANDRO MAYORKAS

IN THE HOT SEAT

Charting the Course of American
History with the First Cabinet
Impeachment in 150 Years

FREEMAN TRENDS

1: Introduction

The impeachment process is a procedure intended to preserve the integrity of government and promote the principles of justice, and it is regarded as a beacon of accountability in the annals of American democracy. With the House of Representatives on the verge of this grave responsibility once more, attention is now focused on the vote to remove Homeland Security Secretary Alejandro Mayorkas from office. An in-depth analysis of the history, importance, and implications of this historic move is necessary at this crucial juncture.

The history of the House of Representatives' vote to impeach

Equipped with the constitutional ability to remove federal officials from office, the House of Representatives is prepared to employ this enormous authority. The actions of Alejandro Mayorkas, the secretary of homeland security, are key to this historic decision. Overseeing one of the most important federal departments, Mayorkas's tenure has been clouded by accusations of misconduct, incapacity, and neglect of duty.

This impeachment vote has its roots in a long list of scandals that have rocked the Department of Homeland Security (DHS) under Mayorkas's direction. The effectiveness and integrity of our country's homeland defense have come under serious scrutiny due to the department's administration under Mayorkas, from the mishandling of immigration policies to the systematic flaws in national security standards.

Furthermore, the public's confidence in Mayorkas's leadership has been severely damaged by recent disclosures surrounding his alleged involvement in nepotism and political favoritism. The DHS's accountability and openness are under threat due to allegations of quid pro quo agreements, conflicts of interest, and unethical behavior.

Importance of Alejandro Mayorkas, the Secretary of Homeland Security, Being Impeached

The importance of Alejandro Mayorkas, the secretary of homeland security, being impeached goes beyond party politics and touches on the essence of our democratic ideals and the necessity of holding public servants responsible for their deeds. Not only is one person's destiny in jeopardy, but also the integrity of our institutions and the importance of the rule of law.

Impeachment is first and foremost a powerful reminder that nobody is above the law, no matter how powerful or powerful they may be. The House of Representatives confirms its commitment to the notion of governmental accountability and sends a strong message that public workers must be held to the highest levels of ethical conduct and performance by putting Mayorkas through the rigors of impeachment proceedings.

Mayorkas' impeachment is a critical step in rebuilding public trust in the Department of Homeland Security and reinforcing the agency's mandate to protect the safety and security of the American people. Amidst unparalleled obstacles, such as the imminent threat of terrorism and the unrelenting assault of cyberattacks, the DHS cannot afford to have a head whose qualifications and moral character are questioned.

Furthermore, the vote to remove Mayorkas from office acts as a wake-up call for reform in the halls of power, forcing decision-makers to address the institutional flaws and systemic failings that have allowed misconduct to grow unchecked. It emphasizes how important it is to have more accountability, transparency, and oversight when using executive authority to make sure the public interest always comes first in all decisions made by the government.

The decision in the House of Representatives to remove Homeland Security Secretary Alejandro Mayorkas from office is not just a political show; it is a turning point in the history of American democracy. It is evidence of the enduring values of accountability, fairness, and the rule of law that serve as the cornerstones of the government of our country. The House must answer the call of history as it considers this important choice and continue to protect the principles that this great republic was built upon, standing as defenders of the public trust.

2: Historical Context of Cabinet Member Impeachment

One important and frequently disputed part of governmental accountability is the removal of cabinet members. The impeachment process, which has its roots in the fundamental ideas of checks and balances, acts as a means of holding powerful individuals responsible for wrongdoing and abuse of authority. Cabinet member impeachment has been a historical problem for several administrations, with each experience providing a different perspective on the interplay of law, power, and governance. We explore the historical background of the impeachment of cabinet members, look at significant prior cases, and make comparisons to other impeachment proceedings in this thorough analysis.

The Impeachment of a Cabinet Member in Historical Context

The idea of impeachment dates back to the time when authorities and kings were subject to a variety of legal remedies to hold them accountable for their deeds. The impeachment procedure was established by the founders of the US Constitution as a crucial instrument for preserving the integrity of the executive branch in the modern era. The President, Vice President, and other civil officers, including cabinet members, may be impeached and removed by Congress under Article II, Section 4 of the Constitution if they are found guilty of "Treason, Bribery, or other high Crimes and Misdemeanors."

The impeachment of cabinet members has been a relatively uncommon but noteworthy event in American history. One of the first was in 1876, when William Belknap, the Secretary of War under President Ulysses S. Grant, was charged with impeachment due to his role in a corruption scandal. Belknap's case established a precedent for holding cabinet members responsible for unethical behavior, highlighting how crucial it is to uphold moral principles in the executive branch.

An Overview of Past Impeachments of Cabinet Members

Belknap and several other cabinet members have been the subject of impeachment cases at some point in American history. During the Nixon administration, Attorney General John Mitchell was connected to the Watergate crisis in one noteworthy case.

Even though Mitchell finally resigned before formal allegations of impeachment were brought against him, his involvement showed that high-ranking officials may be held responsible for criminal behavior.

President Andrew Johnson's 1868 impeachment of Secretary of War Edwin Stanton is another noteworthy case. Stanton was impeached by the House of Representatives as a result of Johnson's decision to remove him from office without Senate permission; nevertheless, he was cleared by a single vote in the Senate. Stanton's case highlighted the need to follow constitutional procedures as well as the delicate balance of power between the legislative and executive branches.

Relative to Previous Impeachment Proceedings

There are a few significant parallels and discrepancies between the impeachments of former cabinet members and other impeachment cases. The fundamental idea of accountability, according to which public servants are held accountable for actions that erode public confidence, is one thing they all have in common. In cases involving cabinet members and other high-ranking officials, the grounds for impeachment are always the same—bribery, corruption, or abuse of power.

But there are also many distinctions, especially in the political context of each impeachment case. The results of impeachment procedures are frequently influenced by partisan differences, as evidenced by the impeachments of Presidents Donald Trump, Bill Clinton, and Andrew Johnson. Similar to this, how serious the accusations are seen to be and the political atmosphere of the moment influence how much public and media attention is given to them.

The historical background of the impeachment of cabinet members provides an important context for understanding the intricacies of accountability and government. Even though it happens infrequently, the impeachment of cabinet ministers is an essential tool for maintaining the integrity of the executive branch and the rule of law. We can better comprehend the tenets and procedures that guide the impeachment process by looking at previous cases and making comparisons to other impeachment trials. No matter their position or status, government officials must always be held accountable for their actions by pursuing justice and upholding democratic principles.

3: Allegations Against Homeland Security Secretary Alejandro Mayorkas

The spotlight frequently shines brightly, exposing both noteworthy accomplishments and divisive issues. Alejandro Mayorkas, the secretary of homeland security, is one such person who is under close examination. Discussions about the nature of the accusations, their potential legal repercussions, and their ethical implications have been triggered by the accusations made against him. It's crucial to examine the specifics closely and critically to fully comprehend how complicated this problem is.

Nature of Allegations

The charges leveled against Secretary Mayorkas are numerous and include mishandling delicate immigration problems in addition to charges of political meddling and favoritism. The most prominent claim is that Mayorkas acted improperly when serving as director of the US Citizenship and Immigration Services (USCIS) by pressuring officials to expedite visa applications for those with political connections. Concerns over the integrity of the immigration system and the possible decline in public confidence in governmental institutions have been raised by these accusations.

Moreover, allegations have been made concerning Mayorkas' participation in the EB-5 visa initiative, which awards green cards to foreign investors who provide a significant sum of money to enterprises that create jobs in the United States. Opponents claim that Mayorkas interfered with several EB-5 applications during the adjudication process, perhaps jeopardizing the program's integrity and eroding the values of justice and openness.

Consequences for Law

Legally speaking, there are concerns regarding possible ethical transgressions and power abuse about the accusations made against Secretary Mayorkas. Such acts might violate federal regulations governing government officials' conduct if they are proven to be true. Laws about bribery, corruption, and conflicts of interest may also be implicated by claims of political favoritism and undue influence.

If Secretary Mayorkas broke any laws or moral standards, these claims must be looked at thoroughly. Mayorkas' career and reputation may be severely impacted by the legal ramifications, which could vary from administrative punishments to criminal prosecution, contingent on the results.

Implications for Ethics

The accusations made against Secretary Mayorkas have important ethical ramifications that extend beyond the legal domain and impact the entire field of public service. The accountability principle and the public's expectation that public servants will behave honorably and impartially are at the center of the issue.

Governmental institutions lose credibility and efficacy when there is a breach of ethics. In addition to damaging Secretary Mayorkas's reputation, it raises questions about the honesty of the Department of Homeland Security and the immigration system at large if it is true that he acted unethically.

Furthermore, the public's faith in the democratic process may be further damaged by the seeming lack of accountability in responding to these accusations. It emphasizes how crucial it is to have strong supervision procedures in place as well as how accountable and transparent governance must be.

The accusations leveled against Alejandro Mayorkas, the secretary of homeland security, go right to the heart of the moral and legal foundation of our democracy. The standards of due process and impartiality must be upheld as investigations progress and evidence is examined. The results of these inquiries will not only dictate

Secretary Mayorkas's future; they will also act as a yardstick for our government's institutions' honesty and dedication to maintaining moral principles in public service. As we navigate these choppy waters, we have to keep going after the truth, justice, and responsibility.

4: House of Representatives Decision to Impeach

Alejandro Mayorkas, the secretary of homeland security, was impeached by the House of Representatives recently, marking a significant step in a politically charged and scrutinized environment. This extraordinary action shook the nation's conscience and caused heated arguments to erupt throughout the corridors of power. Examining the complexities of the impeachment procedure, the slim margin of victory, and the numerous elements that impacted this momentous decision is essential when the dust settles and the decision's effects become apparent.

The central claim in this dispute is Secretary Mayorkas' alleged misbehavior and duty-related neglect. Critics argue that he did not handle important national security problems to the level required of a senior official tasked with protecting the country. The stakes are extremely high, with issues ranging from cyber threats and internal extremism to border security concerns. Any lack of leadership is not acceptable.

It was not decided to impeach Secretary Mayorkas lightly. It took place against a backdrop of extreme partisanship and enduring ideological divisions, which have come to define the political environment more and more. Every vote matters in a situation this divisive, and the impeachment vote's small margin demonstrated the seriousness of the choice and the depth of the discussions.

The House of Representatives' decision to impeach Secretary Mayorkas was influenced by a wide range of factors. First, there's the issue of responsibility and accountability. Secretary Mayorkas is required to carry out his responsibilities with steadfast commitment and skill as a crucial architect of the country's security infrastructure. The integrity of the office is compromised and public trust is eroded by any perception of ineptitude or negligence.

Secondly, issues with honesty and transparency in governance exist. There are significant concerns over the department's integrity under Secretary Mayorkas's direction due to allegations of improper behavior and favoritism in the implementation of Homeland Security policies. These kinds of accusations cannot be readily dismissed in a democracy that was built on the foundations of accountability and transparency.

Thirdly, maintaining democratic values and constitutional standards is essential. The impeachment procedure is an essential tool for maintaining the constitutionally mandated checks and balances and keeping public leaders accountable. Members of the House of Representatives carry out their responsibility to the American people by using their oversight authority to make sure that no person, no matter how powerful, is above the law.

Furthermore, the impeachment narrative also heavily weighs geopolitical factors. Key national security officials' competency and reputation are critical in a world where geopolitical rivalries and rising threats are causing instability. The Department of Homeland Security's leadership may be perceived as weak or unstable, which might have a significant impact on the country's security posture and international reputation.

It is critical to understand that the choice to remove Secretary Mayorkas from office represents larger systemic problems that call for investigation and change in addition to the personal failings of one person. The Department of Homeland Security is confronted with a wide range of intricate issues, ranging from political meddling and institutional lethargy to bureaucratic inefficiency. Bipartisan cooperation, strategic forethought, and an unwavering dedication to the common good are necessary to meet these problems.

One thing is becoming very evident as the impeachment process moves along and the country deals with its ramifications: maintaining the integrity and effectiveness of our homeland security infrastructure is crucial. No matter how one feels about politics or ideologies, the safety and welfare of the American people must always come first. The House of Representatives has sent a strong statement about the value of leadership, responsibility, and loyalty to democratic norms by making Secretary Mayorkas answerable for his conduct. All parties involved now have a responsibility to pay attention to this warning and seek to create a future that is more robust and safe for future generations.

5: Reaction and Response

Homeland Security Secretary Alejandro Mayorkas has shown himself to be a resolute leader in the face of mounting security threats and difficulties, skillfully negotiating the difficulties of securing the country's borders and guaranteeing the safety and security of its residents. A combination of strategic thinking, decisive action, and steadfast dedication to preserving the ideals of justice and protection have characterized Mayorkas's response to these pressing concerns.

As soon as Mayorkas took over as Secretary of Homeland Security, he got to work solving the department's many problems. Having a thorough awareness of how security threats change over time, he moved quickly to bolster cybersecurity infrastructure, improve border security, and fight transnational crime. The nation's defenses have been strengthened and possible hazards have been reduced thanks in large part to Mayorkas's proactive attitude to tackling these challenges.

The foundation of Mayorkas's approach has been his dedication to promoting cooperation and teamwork on a national and worldwide level. Having come to understand the interdependence of security concerns, he has dedicated his time to fostering collaborations with foreign counterparts, law enforcement agencies, and other government agencies. Mayorkas has been able to increase Homeland Security's operational performance and better address new threats by utilizing the group's resources and collective knowledge. In addition, Mayorkas has proven that he is unwaveringly committed to preserving humanity and compassion in the department's enforcement actions. He has pushed for measures that put vulnerable population protection ahead of border security in the face of humanitarian disasters like the migration wave at the southern border. Mayorkas is commended for his pragmatism and sensitivity because of his balanced approach, which demonstrates a deep awareness of the intricacies involved in immigration and border management.

Official Government Reactions

All party stripes of government officials have largely endorsed Mayorkas's leadership. Congressmen of both parties have praised his dedication to collaboration and his proactive approach to addressing security concerns. Republican lawmakers in particular have praised Mayorkas for his efforts to find common ground on divisive matters like immigration reform and his willingness to participate in productive debate.

Democratic leaders have also endorsed Mayorkas's leadership and highlighted his focus on civil liberties and human rights in Homeland Security operations. His efforts to put the reuniting of families split up at the border first and his dedication to enacting just and compassionate immigration laws have received widespread praise.

Furthermore, Mayorkas has established solid alliances with representatives of state and municipal government, realizing the vital role these politicians play in bolstering security on a local level. Through the promotion of cooperation among governors, mayors, and law enforcement agencies, he has enabled the flow of information and resources that are essential for efficiently managing security concerns.

Public Attitude and Media Attention

In the eyes of the general public, Alejandro Mayorkas is a person of skill, moral character, and empathy. According to polls, the majority of Americans think well of him because of his dedication to preserving democratic values and his practical approach to security-related issues. His efforts to maintain a balance between security and civil liberties have been widely commended, with many seeing him as a safeguard against the government's authoritarian tendencies.

The media has generally given Mayorkas's term favorable coverage, emphasizing his calm leadership in the face of chaos. His attempts to resolve persistent issues at the Department of Homeland Security, such as boosting staff morale and expediting bureaucratic procedures, have been highly praised in news reports. Mayorkas has also received recognition for his dedication to transparency and accountability because of his openness to interact with the media and his willingness to be approachable.

As Secretary of Homeland Security, Alejandro Mayorkas has demonstrated proactive leadership, strategic vision, and an unwavering dedication to protecting the security of the country while respecting its principles. Government authorities, the general people, and the media have all praised him for his cooperative style, bipartisan outreach, and commitment to humanitarian ideals. Mayorkas's leadership will surely continue to be essential in guaranteeing the safety and security of the United States and its residents as the challenges of the modern world change.

6: Potential Impacts and Consequences

Alejandro Mayorkas's selection by the Biden administration as Homeland Security Secretary has significant ramifications, effects, and the capacity to change operations and policies in the constantly changing field of national security. Mayorkas has worked for decades in immigration, national security, and law enforcement. He offers a variety of knowledge, viewpoints, and difficulties to the Department of Homeland Security (DHS).

A Brand-New Leadership Era

With Mayorkas taking office, the previous administration's language and policies—which frequently placed a higher priority on border security and immigration restrictions—will change. Mayorkas symbolizes a dedication to inclusivity, diversity, and comprehensive immigration reform as the first immigrant and Latino to lead the DHS. His nomination represents a significant change in direction toward a more humane and practical approach to immigration and national security, in line with President Biden's goals of progress and unification.

Ramifications for immigration laws

Policies about immigration are among the most important areas of influence. Several measures, such as the protection of Dreamers, asylum seekers, and illegal immigrants, are about to be implemented under Mayorkas's leadership to solve the complexity of immigration. His history as the creator of the Deferred Action for Childhood Arrivals (DACA) program demonstrates his commitment to finding reasonable and compassionate answers to the immigration challenge. Mayorkas is expected to strike a careful balance between border security, humanitarian issues, and economic needs; this could result in a more humane and nuanced approach to immigration enforcement.

National Security Strategy Repercussions

Mayorkas takes over an agency that is facing a variety of security risks, such as cyberattacks, domestic extremism, and international criminality. Recalibrating the DHS's strategic priorities to face new threats while defending democratic ideals and civil liberties is his challenge. Mayorkas has the chance to improve interagency cooperation, forge stronger ties with foreign allies, and increase the country's resilience against changing security threats by utilizing his experience in cybersecurity and counterterrorism.

The Agenda of the Biden Administration

Mayorkas's leadership is consistent with the Biden administration's overarching goal, which prioritizes human rights, diplomacy, and multilateralism in the process of making decisions on national security. His dedication to maintaining democratic institutions, protecting the rule of law, and promoting international collaboration is indicative of the administration's attempts to elevate the United States of America's profile in the world. As a principal designer of the administration's immigration policies, Mayorkas is essential to the advancement of comprehensive reforms that improve border security, tackle the underlying reasons for migration, and foster social and economic stability in the Americas.

Impacts on Operations Related to Homeland Security

Mayorkas's leadership is anticipated to improve accountability and transparency, expedite procedures, and spark organizational improvements inside the DHS. To improve information sharing, modernize DHS operations, and increase the efficacy of cybersecurity, disaster response, and border enforcement,

Mayorkas hopes to cultivate an innovative and collaborative culture. His focus on professional growth, diversity, and inclusion in the workforce highlights his dedication to creating a strong and adaptable homeland security organization that can counter challenges from the twenty-first century.

Alejandro Mayorkas has substantial influence on the country's immigration laws, interagency cooperation, and security posture in his capacity as Homeland Security Secretary. Managing border issues and fending off new threats are only two of the possibilities and difficulties that have come his way during his term. Through a path based on pragmatism, compassion, and strategic insight, Mayorkas may redefine the goals and objectives of the DHS, further the agenda of the Biden administration, and protect the security and values of the country in an increasingly linked and complicated world.

7: Legal Proceedings and Next Steps

Alejandro Mayorkas, the secretary of homeland security, is the subject of intense scrutiny, controversy, and conjecture, all of which have erupted around his judicial procedures. As the leader of a vital government organization entrusted with maintaining national security, Mayorkas becomes entangled in a convoluted legal drama that could have far-reaching consequences.

The Department of Homeland Security (DHS) is the subject of accusations of misconduct, authority abuse, and possible protocol violations. Regarding Mayorkas's handling of different immigration policies, border security measures, and DHS resource management, accusations have been made.

Political tensions and ideological division have been evident throughout the court procedures, as both lawmakers and pundits have offered their opinions on the case's potential outcomes. While detractors claim that serious concerns about accountability and transparency necessitate a comprehensive inquiry, supporters of Mayorkas feel that he has been unfairly singled out by political opponents looking to subvert the Biden administration's mission.

The future steps for Mayorkas remain unclear while the legal proceedings continue. The results of any future inquiries, hearings, or trials might have a significant impact on his professional life, the Department of Homeland Security, and national security policy as a whole.

Mayorkas has to continue to carry out his responsibilities as Secretary of Homeland Security while navigating the complexities of the legal system in the face of increasing pressure and scrutiny. In the coming days and weeks, his capacity to manage the department well, carry out tactical changes, and handle urgent security issues will be keenly monitored.

Senate Trial Procedures

The Senate trial proceedings involving prominent public figures, such as Homeland Security Secretary Alejandro Mayorkas, provide evidence of the complex mechanisms inside the American political system. The Senate is crucial in conducting in-depth investigations, holding hearings, and eventually deciding the accused's fate when accusations of impropriety or wrongdoing occur.

The Senate Judiciary Committee, whose duties include investigating legal issues and supervising the confirmation procedure for important government appointees, usually starts the procedure. Regarding Mayorkas, it is probable that the Judiciary Committee would have primary responsibility for scrutinizing the accusations made against him, compiling proof, and conducting witness interviews.

Following the committee's inquiry, a full Senate hearing is scheduled, when members can ask direct questions of Mayorkas, provide evidence, and discuss the merits of the case. During this phase of the process, facts are rigorously examined, passionate rhetoric is frequently used, and intensive inspection is common.

The Senate will have a chance to vote on whether to move on with a formal trial after the hearing. Should a trial be judged necessary, the proceedings would be similar to those in a court of law, with the Senate jury deliberating after hearing arguments from the prosecution and defense as well as witness cross-examinations.

Senate rules and procedures control the trial's path, guaranteeing impartiality, openness, and respect for the due process norms. The Senate has the final say and can decide to find someone innocent or to impeach and remove them from office.

A pillar of American democracy, the Senate trial processes offer a framework for monitoring, accountability, and the defense of the rule of law. The country will witness the strength of its democratic institutions and the dedication of its leaders to maintaining the values of justice and integrity as the Mayorkas case develops.

Forecasts and Conjectures

As the court case concerning Homeland Security Secretary Alejandro Mayorkas progresses, conjecture and predictions abound. As the case's consequences are unclear and its stakes are high, spectators, pundits, and experts are all keen to provide their perspectives.

Others believe Mayorkas will come out of the hearings unscathed, believing that the accusations of misbehavior will turn out to be false or inadequate to justify taking him out of office. They contend that in the end, his dedication to national security, experience with immigration policy, and record of public service will surpass whatever obstacles he may encounter in the political or judicial arena.

Some, on the other hand, are less positive about Mayorkas's chances because of the gravity of the accusations made against him and the possibility that damning information will come to light as the inquiry progresses. They imply that the prospect of his forced resignation or impeachment is imminent, endangering his term as Secretary of Homeland Security.

There are more general concerns regarding the case's effects on the Department of Homeland Security, the Biden administration, and the direction of national security policy in addition to Mayorkas's immediate ramifications. Some others believe that a drawn-out legal dispute may divert attention from important problems the department is dealing with, like border security, counterterrorism initiatives, and cybersecurity risks.

Others bemoan the divisiveness and deadlock that have come to characterize American politics in recent years and fear the damaging impact of party politics on the integrity of the legal system. They worry that Congress will become even more divided over the Mayorkas issue and that public confidence in governmental institutions will decline.

Ultimately, it is still unclear how Alejandro Mayorkas's legal case will turn out, therefore projections and conjecture need to be balanced against the nuance and volatility of the political system. One thing is certain as the case progresses: the country's eyes are glued to Washington's corridors of power, anticipating the outcome of a judicial drama that could have a significant impact on the future of American democracy.

Conclusion

In conclusion, it is evident that the issues we confront today are not just political but also have a deep connection to upholding the integrity of our institutions and our core values, especially when we consider how historic the impeachment proceedings are and how crucial a role they have played in forming our democracy.

The comment of Secretary Alejandro Mayorkas emphasizes the significance of this point in our country's history. It serves as a reminder that the health and vigor of our democracy depend on the pursuit of justice and accountability. By making people answerable for their deeds, irrespective of their status or power, we uphold the idea that nobody is above the law.

Furthermore, it is critical that we reflect on the past, draw lessons from it, and take proactive measures to protect our democracy from future attacks. To achieve this, we must all work together to protect our democratic institutions, enforce the law, and promote an open and accountable society.

This historic impeachment trial has far-reaching consequences outside of the political sphere. They have significant ramifications for both the future of our country and the global community. The way we react to this moment will determine history's path and the legacy we leave for the next generations.

Liberty, justice, and equality for all are the ideals that bind our country together, and we must not waver in the face of hardship. Our goal must be to create a society that is more equal and inclusive, where each person's rights and dignity are upheld.

Alejandro Mayorkas, the secretary of homeland security, tells us that although the path ahead will be difficult, there will be many opportunities. It is our collective responsibility to take advantage of this opportunity and collaborate to create a more promising future for future generations as well as for ourselves. Because the future of our democracy is at stake, let's rise to the occasion with bravery, conviction, and unshakable commitment.